**Hard Press**

TRIVIA

# By Logan Pearsall Smith

1917

*Bibliographical Note*

Some of these pieces were privately printed at the Chiswick Press in 1902. Others have appeared in the "New Statesman" and "The New Republic," and are here reprinted with the Editors' permission.

**Contents** "You must beware of thinking too much about Style," said my kindly adviser, "or you will become like those fastidious people who polish and polish until there is nothing left."

"Then there really are such people?" I asked, lost in the thought of how much I should like to meet them. But the well-informed lady could give me no precise information about them.

I often hear of them in this tantalizing manner, and perhaps one day I shall get to know them. They sound delightful.

*The Author*

These pieces of moral prose have been written, dear Reader, by a large Carnivorous Mammal, belonging to that suborder of the Animal Kingdom which includes also the Orang-outang, the tusked Gorilla, the Baboon with his bright blue and scarlet bottom, and the long-eared Chimpanzee.

*List of Contents*

# BOOK I

# BOOK II

# BOOK I

*How blest my lot, in these sweet fields assign'd Where Peace and Leisure soothe the tuneful mind.*

*Scott*, of Amwell, *Moral Eclogues* (1773)

## Happiness

Cricketers on village greens, haymakers in the evening sunshine, small boats that sail before the wind—all these create in me the illusion of Happiness, as if a land of cloudless pleasure, a piece of the old Golden World, were hidden, not (as poets have imagined), in far seas or beyond inaccessible mountains, but here close at hand, if one could find it, in some undiscovered valley. Certain grassy lanes seem to lead between the meadows thither; the wild pigeons talk of it behind the woods.

## To-Day

I woke this morning out of dreams into what we call Reality, into the daylight, the furniture of my familiar bedroom—in fact into the well-known, often-discussed, but, to my mind, as yet unexplained Universe.

Then I, who came out of Eternity and seem to be on my way thither, got up and spent the day as I usually spend it. I read, I pottered, I talked, and took exercise; and I sat punctually down to eat the cooked meals that appeared at stated intervals.

## The Afternoon Post

The village Post Office, with its clock and letter-box, its postmistress lost in tales of love-lorn Dukes and coroneted woe, and the sallow-faced grocer watching from his window opposite, is the scene of a daily crisis in my life, when every afternoon I walk there through the country lanes and ask that well-read young lady for my letters. I always expect good news and cheques; and then, of course, there is the magical Fortune which is coming, and word of it may reach me any day. What it is, this strange Felicity, or whence it shall come, I have no notion; but I hurry down in the morning to find the news on the breakfast table, open telegrams in delighted panic, and say to myself "Here it is!" when at night I hear wheels approaching along the road. So, happy in the hope of Happiness, and not greatly concerned with any other interest or ambition, I live on in my quiet, ordered house; and so I shall live perhaps until the end. Is it, indeed, merely the last great summons and revelation for which I am waiting? I do not know.

## The Busy Bees

Sitting for hours idle in the shade of an apple tree, near the garden-hives, and under the aerial thoroughfares of those honey-merchants—sometimes when the noonday heat is loud with their minute industry, or when they fall in crowds out of the late sun to their night-long labours-I have sought instruction from the Bees, and tried to appropriate to myself the old industrious lesson.

And yet, hang it all, who by rights should be the teachers and who the learners? For those peevish, over-toiled, utilitarian insects, was there no lesson to be derived from the spectacle of Me? Gazing out at me with myriad eyes from their joyless factories, might they not learn at last—might I not finally teach them—a wiser and more generous-hearted way to improve the shining hour?

## The Wheat

The Vicar, whom I met once or twice in my walks about the fields, told me that he was glad that I was taking an interest in farming. Only my feeling about wheat, he said, puzzled him.

Now the feeling in regard to wheat which I had not been able to make clear to the Vicar was simply one of amazement. Walking one day into a field that I had watched yellowing beyond the trees, I found myself dazzled by the glow and great expanse of gold. I bathed myself in the intense yellow under the intense blue sky; how dim it made the oak trees and copses and all the rest of the English landscape seem! I had not remembered the glory of the Wheat; nor imagined in my reading that in a country so far from the Sun there could be anything so rich, so prodigal, so reckless, as this opulence of ruddy gold, bursting out from the cracked earth as from some fiery vein below. I remembered how for thousands of years Wheat had been the staple of wealth, the hoarded wealth of famous cities and empires; I thought of the processes of corn-growing, the white oxen ploughing, the great barns, the winnowing fans, the mills with the splash of their wheels, or arms slow-turning in the wind; of cornfields at harvest-time, with shocks and sheaves in the glow of sunset, or under the sickle moon; what beauty it brought into the northern landscape, the antique, passionate, Biblical beauty of the South!

## The Coming of Fate

When I seek out the sources of my thoughts, I find they had their beginning in fragile Chance; were born of little moments that shine for me curiously in the past. Slight the impulse that made me take this turning at the crossroads, trivial and fortuitous the meeting, and light as gossamer the thread that first knit me to my friend. These are full of wonder; more mysterious are the moments that must have brushed me with their wings and passed me by: when Fate beckoned and I did not see it, when new Life trembled for a second on the threshold; but the word was not spoken, the hand was not held out, and the Might-have-been shivered and vanished, dim as a into the waste realms of non-existence.

11

So I never lose a sense of the whimsical and perilous charm of daily life, with its meetings and words and accidents. Why, to-day, perhaps, or next week, I may hear a voice, and, packing up my Gladstone bag, follow it to the ends of the world.

*My Speech*

"Ladies and Gentlemen," I began—The Vicar was in the chair; Mrs. La Mountain and her daughters sat facing us; and in the little schoolroom, with its maps and large Scripture prints, its blackboard with the day's sums still visible on it, were assembled the labourers of the village, the old family coachman and his wife, the one-eyed postman, and the gardeners and boys from the Hall. Having culled from the newspapers a few phrases, I had composed a speech which I delivered with a spirit and eloquence surprising even to myself, and which was now enthusiastically received. The Vicar cried "Hear, Hear!", the Vicar's wife pounded her umbrella with such emphasis, and the villagers cheered so heartily, that my heart was warmed. I began to feel the meaning of my own words; I beamed on the audience, felt that they were all brothers, all wished well to the Republic; and it seemed to me an occasion to express my real ideas and hopes for the Commonwealth.

Brushing therefore to one side, and indeed quite forgetting my safe principles, I began to refashion and new-model the State. Most existing institutions were soon abolished; and then, on their ruins, I proceeded to build up the bright walls and palaces of the City within me—the City I had read of in Plato. With enthusiasm, and, I flatter myself, with eloquence, I described it all—the Warriors, that race of golden youth bred from the State-ordered embraces of the brave and fair; those philosophic Guardians, who, being ever accustomed to the highest and most extensive views, and thence contracting an habitual greatness, possessed the truest fortitude, looking down indeed with a kind of disregard on human life and death. And then, declaring that the pattern of this City was laid up in Heaven, I sat down, amid the cheers of the uncomprehending little audience.

And afterward, in my rides about the country, when I saw on walls and the doors of barns, among advertisements of sales, or regulations about birds' eggs or the movements of swine, little weather-beaten, old-looking notices on which it was stated that I would "address the meeting," I remembered how the walls and towers of the City I had built up in that little schoolroom had shone with no heavenly light in the eyes of the Vicar's party.

*Stonehenge*

They sit there forever on the dim horizon of my mind, that Stonehenge circle of elderly disapproving Faces—Faces of the Uncles and Schoolmasters and Tutors who frowned on my youth.

In the bright centre and sunlight I leap, I caper, I dance my dance; but when I look up, I see they are not deceived. For nothing ever placates them, nothing ever moves to a look of approval that ring of bleak and contemptuous Faces.

12

Battling my way homeward one dark night against the wind and rain, a sudden gust, stronger than the others, drove me back into the shelter of a tree. But soon the Western sky broke open; the illumination of the Stars poured down from behind the dispersing clouds.

I was astonished at their brightness, to see how they filled the night with their soft lustre. So I went my way accompanied by them; Arcturus followed me, and becoming entangled in a leafy tree, shone by glimpses, and then emerged triumphant, Lord of the Western sky. Moving along the road in the silence of my own footsteps, my thoughts were among the Constellations. I was one of the Princes of the starry Universe; in me also there was something that was not insignificant and mean and of no account.

*Silvia Doria*

Beyond the blue hills, within riding distance, there is a country of parks and beeches, with views of the far-off sea. I remember in one of my rides coming on the place which was the scene of the pretty, old-fashioned story of Silvia Doria. Through the gates, with fine gate-posts, on which heraldic beasts, fierce and fastidious, were upholding coroneted shields, I could see, at the end of the avenue, the faade of the House, with its stone pilasters, and its balustrade on the steep roof.

More than one hundred years ago, in that Park, with its Italianized house, and level gardens adorned with statues and garden temples, there lived, they say, an old Lord with his two handsome sons. The old Lord had never ceased mourning for his Lady, though she had died a good many years before; there were no neighbours he visited, and few strangers came inside the great Park walls. One day in Spring, however, just when the apple trees had burst into blossom, the gilded gates were thrown open, and a London chariot with prancing horses drove up the Avenue. And in the chariot, smiling and gay, and indeed very beautiful in her dress of yellow silk, and her great Spanish hat with drooping feathers, sat Silvia Doria, come on a visit to her cousin, the old Lord.

It was her father who had sent her—that he might be more free, some said, to pursue his own wicked courses—while others declared that he intended her to marry the old Lord's eldest son.

In any case, Silvia Doria came like the Spring, like the sunlight, into the lonely place. Even the old Lord felt himself curiously happy when he heard her voice singing about the house; as for Henry and Francis, it was heaven for them just to walk by her side down the garden alleys.

And Silvia Doria, though hitherto she had been but cold toward the London gallants who had courted her, found, little by little, that her heart was not untouched.

But, in spite of her father, and her own girlish love of gold and rank, it was not for Henry that she cared, not for the old Lord, but for Francis, the younger son. Did Francis know of this? They were secretly lovers, the old scandal reported; and the scandal, it may be, had reached her father's ears.

For one day a coach with foaming horses, and the wicked face of an old man at its window, galloped up the avenue; and soon afterwards, when the coach drove away, Silvia Doria was sitting by the old man's side, sobbing bitterly.

And after she had gone, a long time, many of the old, last-century years, went by without any change. And then Henry, the eldest son, was killed in hunting; and the old Lord dying a few years later, the titles and the great house and all the land and gold came to Francis, the younger son. But after his father's death he was but seldom there; having, as it seemed, no love for the place, and living for the most part abroad and alone, for he never married.

And again, many years went by. The trees grew taller and darker about the house; the yew hedges unclipt now, hung their branches over the moss-grown paths; ivy almost smothered the statues; and the plaster fell away in great patches from the discoloured garden temples.

But at last one day a chariot drove up to the gates; a footman pulled at the crazy bell, telling the gate-keeper that his mistress wished to visit the Park. So the gates creaked open, the chariot glittered up the avenue to the deserted place; and a lady stepped out, went into the garden, and walked among its moss-grown paths and statues. As the chariot drove out again, "Tell your Lord," the lady said, smiling, to the lodge-keeper, "that Silvia Doria came back."

*Bligh House*

To the West, in riding past the walls of Bligh, I remembered an incident in the well-known siege of that house, during the Civil Wars: How, among Waller's invading Roundhead troops, there happened to be a young scholar, a poet and lover of the Muses, fighting for the cause, as he thought, of ancient Freedom, who, one day, when the siege was being more hotly urged, pressing forward and climbing a wall, suddenly found himself in a quiet old garden by the house. And here, for a time forgetting, as it would seem, the battle, and heedless of the bullets that now and then flew past him like peevish wasps, the young Officer stayed, gathering roses—old-fashioned damask roses, streaked with red and white—which, for the sake of a Court Beauty, there besieged with her father, he carried to the house; falling, however, struck by a chance bullet, or shot perhaps by one of his own party. A few of the young Officer's verses, written in the stilted fashion of the time, and almost unreadable now, have been preserved. The lady's portrait hangs in the white drawing room at Bligh; a simpering, faded figure, with ringlets and drop-pearls, and a dress of amber-coloured silk.

*In Church*

"For the Pen," said the Vicar; and in the sententious pause that followed, I felt that I would offer any gifts of gold to avert or postpone the solemn, inevitable, hackneyed, and yet, as it seemed to me, perfectly appalling statement that "the Pen is mightier than the Sword."

## Parsons

All the same I like Parsons; they think nobly of the Universe, and believe in Souls and Eternal Happiness. And some of them, I am told, believe in Angels—that there are Angels who guide our footsteps, and flit to and fro unseen on errands in the air about us.

## The Sound of a Voice

As the thoughtful Baronet talked, as his voice went on sounding in my ears, all the light of desire, and of the sun, faded from the Earth; I saw the vast landscape of the world dim, as in an eclipse; its populations eating their bread with tears, its rich men sitting listless in their palaces, and aged Kings crying "Vanity, Vanity, all is Vanity!" lugubriously from their thrones.

## What Happens

"Yes," said Sir Thomas, speaking of a modern novel, "it certainly does seem strange; but the novelist was right. Such things do happen."

"But my dear Sir," I burst out, in the rudest manner, "think what life is—just think what really happens! Why people suddenly swell up and turn dark purple; they hang themselves on meat-hooks; they are drowned in horse-ponds, are run over by butchers' carts, and are burnt alive and cooked like mutton chops!"

## A Precaution

The folio gave at length philosophic consolations for all the ills and misfortunes said by the author to be inseparable from human existence—Poverty, Shipwreck, Plague, Love-Deceptions, and Inundations. Against these antique Disasters I armed my soul; and I thought it as well to prepare myself against another inevitable ancient calamity called "Cornutation," or by other less learned names. How Philosophy taught that after all it was but a pain founded on conceit, a blow that hurt not; the reply of the Cynic philosopher to one who reproached him, "Is it my fault or hers?"; how Nevisanus advises the sufferer to ask himself if he have not offended; Jerome declares it impossible to prevent; how few or none are safe, and the inhabitants of some countries, especially parts of Africa, consider it the usual and natural thing; How Cæsar, Pompey, Augustus, Agamemnon, Menelaus, Marcus Aurelius, and many other great Kings and Princes had all worn Actaeon's badge; and how Philip turned it to a jest, Pertinax the Emperor made no reckoning of it; Erasmus declared it was best winked at, there being no remedy but patience, *Dies dolorem minuit*; Time,

Age must mend it; and how according to the best authorities, bars, bolts, oaken doors, and towers of brass, are all in vain. "She is a woman," as the old Pedant wrote to a fellow Philosopher....

## The Great Work

Sitting, pen in hand, alone in the stillness of the library, with flies droning behind the sunny blinds, I considered in my thoughts what should be the subject of my great Work. Should I complain against the mutability of Fortune, and impugn Fate and the Constellations; or should I reprehend the never-satisfied heart of querulous Man, drawing elegant contrasts between the unsullied snow of mountains, the serene shining of stars, and our hot, feverish lives and foolish repinings? Or should I confine myself to denouncing contemporary Vices, crying "Fie!" on the Age with Hamlet, sternly unmasking its hypocrisies, and riddling through and through its comfortable Optimisms?

Or with Job, should I question the Universe, and puzzle my sad brains about Life—the meaning of Life on this apple-shaped Planet?

## My Mission

But when in modern books, reviews, and thoughtful magazines I read about the Needs of the Age, its Complex Questions. its Dismays, Doubts, and Spiritual Agonies, I feel an impulse to go out and comfort it, to still its cries, and speak earnest words of Consolation to it.

## The Birds

But how can one toil at the great task with this hurry and tumult of birds just outside the open window? I hear the Thrush, and the Blackbird, that romantic liar; then the delicate cadence, the wiry descending scale of the Willow-wren, or the Blackcap's stave of mellow music. All these are familiar—but what is that unknown voice, that thrilling note? I hurry out; the voice flees and I follow; and when I return and sit down again to my task, the Yellowhammer trills his sleepy song in the noonday heat; the drone of the Greenfinch lulls me into dreamy meditations. Then suddenly from his tree-trunks and forest recesses comes the Green Woodpecker, and mocks at me an impudent voice full of liberty and laughter.

Why should all the birds of the air conspire against me? My concern is with the sad Human Species, with lapsed and erroneous Humanity, not with that inconsiderate, wandering, feather-headed race.

## High Life

Although that immense Country House was empty and for sale, and I had got an order to view it, I needed all my courage to walk through the lordly gates, and up the avenue, and then to ring the door-bell. And when I was ushered in, and the shutters were removed to let the daylight into those vast apartments, I sneaked through them, cursing the dishonest curiosity which had brought me into a place where I had no business. But I was treated with such deference, and so plainly regarded as a possible purchaser, that I soon began to believe in the opulence imputed to me. From all the novels describing the mysterious and glittering life of the Great which I had read (and I had read many), there came to me the enchanting vision of my own existence in this Palace. I filled the vast spaces with the shine of jewels and stir of voices; I saw a vision of ladies sweeping in their tiaras down the splendid stairs.

But my Soul, in her swell of pride, soon outgrew these paltry limits, O no! Never could I box up and house and localize under that lowly roof the Magnificence and Ostentation of which I was capable.

Then for one thing there was stabling for only forty horses; and of course, as I told them, this would never do.

*Empty Shells*

They lie like empty seashells on the shores of Time, the old worlds which the spirit of man once built for his habitation, and then abandoned. Those little earth-centred, heaven-encrusted universes of the Greeks and Hebrews seem quaint enough to us, who have formed, thought by thought from within, the immense modern Cosmos in which we live—the great Creation of granite, planned in such immeasurable proportions, and moved by so pitiless a mechanism, that it sometimes appals even its own creators. The rush of the great rotating Sun daunts us; to think to the distance of the fixed stars cracks our brain.

But if the ephemeral Being who has imagined these eternal spheres and spaces, must dwell almost as an alien in their icy vastness, yet what a splendour lights up for him and dazzles in those great halls! Anything less limitless would be now a prison; and he even dares to think beyond their boundaries, to surmise that he may one day outgrow this vast Mausoleum, and cast from him the material Creation as an integument too narrow for his insolent Mind.

*Dissatisfaction*

For one thing I hate Spiders—I dislike all kinds of Insects. Their cold intelligence, their empty, stereotyped, unremitted industry repel me. And I am not altogether happy about the future of the Human Race; when I think of the slow refrigeration of the Earth, the Sun's waning, and the ultimate, inevitable collapse of the Solar System, I have grave misgivings. And all the books I have read and forgotten-the thought that my mind is really nothing but a sieve—this, too, at times disheartens me.

*A Fancy*

More than once, though, I have pleased myself with the notion that somewhere there is good Company which will like this little Book—these Thoughts (if I may call them so) dipped up from that phantasmagoria or phosphorescence which, by some unexplained process of combustion, flickers over the large lump of soft gray matter in the bowl of my skull.

## They

Their taste is exquisite; They live in Georgian houses, in a world of ivory and precious china, of old brickwork and stone pilasters. In white drawing rooms I see Them, or on blue, bird-haunted lawns. They talk pleasantly of me, and their eyes watch me. From the diminished, ridiculous picture of myself which the glass of the world gives me, I turn for comfort, for happiness, to my image in the kindly mirror of those eyes.

Who are They? Where, in what paradise or palace, shall I ever find Them? I may walk all the streets, ring all the door-bells of the World, but I shall never find them. Yet nothing has value for me save In the crown of Their approval; for Their coming—which will never be—I build and plant, and for Them alone I secretly write this little Book, which They will never read.

## In the Pulpit

The Vicar had certain literary tastes; in his youth he had written an *Ode to the Moon*; and he would speak of the difficulty he found in composing his sermons, week after week.

Now I felt that if I composed and preached sermons, I should by no means confine myself to the Vicar's threadbare subjects— should preach the Wrath of God, and sound the Last Trump in the ears of my Hell-doomed congregation, cracking the heavens and dissolving the earth with the eclipses and thunders and earthquakes of the Day of Judgment. Then I might refresh them with high and incomprehensible Doctrines, beyond the reach of Reason—Predestination, Election, the Co-existences and Co-eternities of the incomprehensible Triad. And with what a holy vehemence would I exclaim and cry out against all forms of doctrinal Error—all the execrable hypotheses of the great Heresiarchs! Then there would be many ancient and learned and out-of-the-way Iniquities to denounce, and splendid, neglected Virtues to inculcate—Apostolic Poverty, and Virginity, that precious jewel, that fair garland, so prized in Heaven, but so rare on earth.

For in the range of creeds and morals it is the highest peaks that shine for me with a certain splendour: it is toward those radiant Alps that, if I were a Clergyman, I would lead my flock to pasture.

## Human Ends

18

I really was impressed, as we paced up and down the avenue, by the Vicar's words and weighty, weighed advice. He spoke of the various professions; mentioned contemporaries of his own who had achieved success: how one had a Seat in Parliament, would be given a Seat in the Cabinet when his party next came in; another was a Bishop with a Seat in the House of Lords; a third was a Barrister who was soon, it was said, to be raised to the Bench.

But in spite of my good intentions, my real wish to find, before it is too late, some career or other for myself (and the question is getting serious), I am far too much at the mercy of ludicrous images. Front Seats, Episcopal, Judicial, Parliamentary Benches—were all the ends then, I asked my self, of serious, middle-aged ambition only things to sit on?

## Lord Arden

"If I were Lord Arden," said the Vicar, "I should shut up that great House; it's too big—what can a young unmarried man...?"

"If I were Lord Arden," said the Vicar's wife (and Mrs. La Mountain's tone showed how much she disapproved of that young Nobleman), "if I were Lord Arden, I should live there, and do my duty to my tenants and neighbours."

"If I were Lord Arden," I said; but then it flashed vividly into my mind, suppose I really were this opulent young Lord? I quite forgot to whom I was talking; my memory was occupied with the names of people who had been famous for their enormous pleasures; who had filled their Palaces with guilty revels, and built Pyramids, Obelisks, and half-acre Tombs, to soothe their Pride. My mind kindled at the thought of these Audacities. "If I were Lord Arden!" I cried....

## The Starry Heaven

"But what are they really? What do they say they are?" the small young lady asked me. We were looking up at the Stars, which were quivering that night in splendid hosts above the lawns and trees.

So I tried to explain some of the views that have been held about them. How people first of all had thought them mere candles set in the sky, to guide their own footsteps when the Sun was gone; till wise men, sitting on the Chaldean plains, and watching them with aged eyes, became impressed with the solemn view that those still and shining lights were the executioners of God's decrees, and irresistible instruments of His Wrath; and that they moved fatally among their celestial Houses to ordain and set out the fortunes and misfortunes of each race of newborn mortals. And so it was believed that every man or woman had, from the cradle, fighting for or against him or her, some great Star, Formalhaut, perhaps, Aldebaran, Altar: while great Heroes and Princes were more splendidly attended, and marched out to their forgotten battles with troops and armies of heavenly Constellations.

But this noble old view was not believed in now; the Stars were no longer regarded as malignant or beneficent Powers; and I explained how most serious people thought that somewhere—though just where they did not know—above the vault of Sky, was to be found the final home of earnest men and women; where, as a reward for their right views and conduct, they were to rejoice forever, wearing those diamonds of the starry night arranged in glorious crowns. This notion, however, had been disputed by Poets and Lovers: it was Love, according to these young astronomers, that moved the Sun and other Stars; the Constellations being heavenly palaces, where people who had adored each other were to meet and live always together after Death.

Then I spoke of the modern and real immensity of the unfathomed Skies. But suddenly the vast meaning of my words rushed into my mind; I felt myself dwindling, falling through the blue. And yet, in these silent seconds, there thrilled through me in the cool sweet air and night no chill of death or nothingness; but the taste and joy of this Earth, this orchard-plot of earth, floating unknown, far away in unfathomed space, with its Moon and meadows.

## My Map

The "Known World" I called the map which I amused myself making for the children's schoolroom. It included France, England, Italy, Greece, and all the old shores of the Mediterranean; but the rest I marked "Unknown"; sketching into the East the doubtful realms of Ninus and Semiramis; changing back Germany into the Hyrcanian Forest; and drawing pictures of the supposed inhabitants of these unexplored regions, Dog-Apes, Satyrs, Cannibals, and Misanthropes, Cimmerians involved in darkness, Amazons, and Headless Men. And all around the Map I coiled the coils, and curled the curling waves of the great Sea *Oceanum*, with the bursting cheeks of the four Winds, blowing from the four imagined hinges of the Universe.

## The Snob

As I paced in fine company on that Terrace, I felt chosen, exempt, and curiously happy. There was a glamour in the air, a something in the special flavour of that moment that was like the consciousness of Salvation, or the smell of ripe peaches on a sunny wall.

I know what you're going to call me, Reader. But I am not to be bullied and abashed by words. And after all, why not let oneself be dazzled and enchanted? Are not Illusions pleasant, and is this a world in which Romance hangs on every tree?

And how about your own life? Is that, then, so full of golden visions?

## Companions

Dearest, prettiest, and sweetest of my retinue, who gather with delicate industry bits of silk and down from the bleak world to make the soft nest of my fatuous repose;

20

who ever whisper honied words in my ear, or trip before me holding up deceiving mirrors—is it Hope, or is it not rather Vanity, that I love the best?

## Edification

"I must really improve my Mind," I tell myself, and once more begin to patch and repair that crazy structure. So I toil and toil on at the vain task of edification, though the wind tears off the tiles, the floors give way, the ceilings fall, strange birds build untidy nests in the rafters, and owls hoot and laugh in the tumbling chimneys.

## The Rose

The old lady had always been proud of the great rose-tree in her garden, and was fond of telling how it had grown from a cutting she had brought years before from Italy, when she was first married. She and her husband had been travelling back in their carriage from Rome (it was before the time of railways), and on a bad piece of road south of Siena they had broken down, and had been forced to pass the night in a little house by the roadside. The accommodation was wretched of course; she had spent a sleepless night, and rising early had stood, wrapped up, at her window, with the cool air blowing on her face, to watch the dawn. She could still, after all these years, remember the blue mountains with the bright moon above them, and how a far-off town on one of the peaks had gradually grown whiter and whiter, till the moon faded, the mountains were touched with the pink of the rising sun, and suddenly the town was lit as by an illumination, one window after another catching and reflecting the sun's beams, till at last the whole little city twinkled and sparkled up in the sky like a nest of stars.

That morning, finding they would have to wait while their carriage was being repaired, they had driven in a local conveyance up to the city on the mountain, where they had been told they would find better quarters; and there they had stayed two or three days. It was one of the miniature Italian cities with a high church, a pretentious piazza, a few narrow streets and little palaces, perched all compact and complete, on the top of a mountain, within an enclosure of walls hardly larger than an English kitchen garden. But it was full of life and noise, echoing all day and all night with the sounds of feet and voices.

The Caf of the simple inn where they stayed was the meeting-place of the notabilities of the little city; the *Sindaco*, the *avvocato*, the doctor, and a few others; and among them they noticed a beautiful, slim, talkative old man, with bright black eyes and snow-white hair—tail and straight and still with the figure of a youth, although the waiter told them with pride that the *Conte* was *molto vecchio*—would in fact be eighty in the following year. He was the last of his family, the waiter added—they had once been great and rich people—but he had no descendants; in fact the waiter mentioned with complacency, as if it were a story on which the locality prided itself, that the *Conte* had been unfortunate in love, and had never married.

21

The old gentleman, however, seemed cheerful enough; and it was plain that he took an interest in the strangers, and wished to make their acquaintance. This was soon effected by the friendly waiter; and after a little talk the old man invited them to visit his villa and garden which were just outside the walls of the town. So the next afternoon, when the sun began to descend, and they saw in glimpses through doorways and windows blue shadows beginning to spread over the brown mountains, they went to pay their visit. It was not much of a place, a small, modernized stucco villa, with a hot pebbly garden, and in it a stone basin with torpid gold fish, and a statue of Diana and her hounds against the wall. But what gave a glory to it was a gigantic rose-tree which clambered over the house, almost smothering the windows, and filling the air with the perfume of its sweetness. Yes, it was a fine rose, the *Conte* said proudly when they praised it, and he would tell the Signora about it. And as they sat there, drinking the wine he offered them, he alluded with the cheerful indifference of old age to his love-affair, as though he took for granted that they had heard of it already.

"The lady lived across the valley there beyond that hill. I was a young man then, for it was many years ago. I used to ride over to see her; it was a long way, but I rode fast, for young men, as no doubt the Signora knows, are impatient. But the lady was not kind, she would keep me waiting, oh, for hours; and one day when I had waited very long I grew very angry, and as I walked up and down in the garden where she had told me she would see me, I broke one of her roses, broke a branch from it; and when I saw what I had done, I hid it inside my coat—so—and when I came home I planted it, and the Signora sees how it has grown. If the Signora admires it, I must give her a cutting to plant also in her garden; I am told the English have beautiful gardens that are green, and not burnt with the sun like ours."

The next day, when their mended carriage had come up to fetch them, and they were just starting to drive away from the inn, the *Conte's* old servant appeared with the rose-cutting neatly wrapped up, and the compliments and wishes for a *buon viaggio* from her master. The town collected to see them depart, and the children ran after their carriage through the gate of the little city. They heard a rush of feet behind them for a few moments, but soon they were far down toward the valley; the little town with all its noise and life was high above them on its mountain peak.

She had planted the rose at home, where it had grown and flourished in a wonderful manner, and every June the great mass of leaves and shoots still broke out into a passionate splendour of scent and scarlet colour, as if in its root and fibres there still burnt the anger and thwarted desire of that Italian lover. Of course the old *Conte* must have died many years ago; she had forgotten his name, and had even forgotten the name of the mountain city that she had stayed in, after first seeing it twinkling at dawn in the sky, like a nest of stars.

*The Vicar of Lynch*

When I heard through country gossip of the strange happening at Lynch which had caused so great a scandal, and led to the disappearance of the deaf old Vicar of that

22

remote village, I collected all the reports I could about it, for I felt that at the centre of this uncomprehending talk and wild anecdote there was something with more meaning than a mere sudden outbreak of blasphemy and madness.

It appeared that the old Vicar, after some years spent in the quiet discharge of his parochial duties, had been noticed to become more and more odd in his appearance and behaviour; and it was also said that he had gradually introduced certain alterations into the Church services. These had been vaguely supposed at the time to be of a High Church character, but afterwards they were put down to a growing mental derangement, which had finally culminated at that notorious Harvest Festival, when his career as a clergyman of the Church of England had ended. On this painful occasion the old man had come into church outlandishly dressed, and had gone through a service with chanted gibberish and unaccustomed gestures, and prayers which were unfamiliar to his congregation. There was also talk of a woman's figure on the altar, which the Vicar had unveiled at a solemn moment in this performance; and I also heard echo of other gossip—gossip that was, however, authoritatively contradicted and suppressed as much as possible—about the use of certain other symbols of a most unsuitable kind. Then a few days after the old man had disappeared—some of the neighbours believed that he was dead; some, that he was now shut up in an asylum for the insane.

Such was the fantastic and almost incredible talk I listened to, but in which, as I say, I found much more meaning than my neighbours. For one thing, although they knew that the Vicar had come from Oxford to this remote College living, they knew nothing of his work and scholarly reputation in that University, and none of them had probably ever heard of—much less read—an important book which he had written, and which was the standard work on his special subject. To them he was simply a deaf, eccentric, and solitary clergyman; and I think I was the only person in the neighbourhood who had conversed with him on the subject concerning which he was the greatest living authority in England.

For I had seen the old man once—curiously enough at the time of a Harvest Festival, though it was some years before the one which had led to his disappearance. Bicycling one day over the hills, I had ridden down into a valley of cornfields, and then, passing along an unfenced road that ran across a wide expanse of stubble, I came, after getting off to open three or four gates, upon a group of thatched cottages, with a little, unrestored Norman church standing among great elms, I left my bicycle and walked through the churchyard, and as I went into the church, through its deeply-recessed Norman doorway, a surprisingly pretty sight met my eyes. The dim, cool, little interior was set out and richly adorned with an abundance of fruit and vegetables, yellow gourds, apples and plums and golden wheat sheaves, great loaves of bread, and garlands of September flowers. A shabby-looking old clergyman was standing on the top of a step-ladder, finishing the decorations, when I entered. As soon as he saw me he came down, and I spoke to him, praising the decorations, and raising my voice a little, for I noticed that he was somewhat deaf. We talked of the Harvest Festival, and as I soon perceived that I was talking with a man of books and University education, I ventured to hint at what had vividly impressed me in that old, gaudily-decorated church—its pagan character, as if it were a rude archaic temple in some corner of the antique world, which had been adorned, two thousand years ago, by pious country folk for some local festival. The old clergyman was not in the least shocked by my remark; it seemed indeed rather to please him; there was, he agreed, something of a pagan character in the modern Harvest Festival—it was no doubt a bit of the old primitive Vegetation Ritual, the old Religion of the soil; a Festival, which, like so many others, had not been destroyed by Christianity, but absorbed into it, and given a new meaning. "Indeed," he added, talking on as if the subject interested him, and expressing himself with a certain donnish carefulness of speech that I found pleasant to listen to, "the Harvest Festival is undoubtedly a survival of the prehistoric worship of that Corn Goddess who, in classical times, was called Demeter and Ioulo and Ceres, but whose cult as an Earth-Mother and Corn-Spirit is of much greater antiquity. For there is no doubt that this Vegetation Spirit has been worshipped from the earliest times by agricultural peoples; the wheat fields and ripe harvests being naturally suggestive of the presence amid the corn of a kindly Being, who, in return for due rites and offerings, will vouchsafe nourishing rains and golden harvests." He mentioned the references in Virgil, and the description in Theocritus of a Sicilian Harvest Festival—these were no doubt familiar to me; but if I was interested in the subject, I should find, he said, much more information collected in a book which he had written, but of which I had probably never heard, about the Vegetation Deities in Greek Religion. As it happened I knew the book, and felt now much interested in my chance meeting with the distinguished author; and after expressing this as best I could, I rode off, promising to visit him again. This promise I was never able to fulfil; but when afterwards, on my return to the neighbourhood, I heard of that unhappy scandal, my memory of this meeting and our talk enabled me to form a theory as to what had really happened.

It seemed plain to me that the change had been too violent for this elderly scholar, taken from his books and college rooms and set down in the solitude of this remote valley, amid the richness and living sap of Nature. The gay spectacle, right under his old eyes, of growing shoots and budding foliage, of blossoming and flowering, and the ripening of fruits and crops, had little by little (such was my theory) unhinged his brains. More and more his thoughts had come to dwell, not on the doctrines of the Church in which he had long ago taken orders, but on the pagan rites which had formed his life-long study, and which had been the expression of a life not unlike the agricultural life amid which he now found himself living. So as his derangement grew upon him in his solitude, he had gradually transformed, with a maniac's cunning, the Christian services, and led his little congregation, all unknown to themselves, back toward their ancestral worship of the Corn-Goddess. At last he had thrown away all disguise, and had appeared as a hierophant of Demeter, dressed in a fawn skin, with a crown of poplar leaves, and pedantically carrying the mystic basket and the winnowing fan appropriate to these mysteries. The wheaten posset he offered the shocked communicants belonged to these also, and the figure of a woman on the altar was of course the holy Wheatsheaf, whose unveiling was the culminating point in that famous ritual.

It is much to be regretted that I could not recover full and more exact details of that celebration in which this great scholar had probably embodied his mature knowledge concerning a subject which has puzzled generations of students. But what powers of careful observation could one expect from a group of labourers and small farmers? Some of the things that reached my ears I refused to believe—the mention of pig's blood for instance, and especially the talk of certain grosser symbols, which the choir boys, it was whispered, had carried about the church in ceremonious procession. Village people have strange imaginations; and to this event, growing more and more monstrous as they talked it over, they must themselves have added this grotesque detail. However, I have written to consult an Oxford authority on this interesting point, and he has been kind enough to explain at length that although at the *Haloa*, or winter festival of the Corn-Goddess, and also at the *Chloeia*, or festival in early spring, some symbolization of the reproductive powers of Nature would be proper and appropriate, it would have been quite out of place at the *Thalysia*, or autumn festival of thanksgiving. I feel certain that a solecism of this nature—the introduction into a particular rite of features not sanctioned by the texts—would have seemed a shocking thing, even to the unhinged mind of one who had always been so careful a scholar.

## Tu Quoque Fontium

Just to sit in the Sun, to bask like an animal in its heat—this is one of my country recreations. And often I reflect what a thing after all it is still to be alive and sitting here, above all the buried people of the world, in the kind and famous Sunshine.

Beyond the orchard there is a place where the stream, hurrying out from under a bridge, makes for itself a quiet pool. A beech-tree upholds its green light over the blue water; and there, when I have grown weary of the sun, the great glaring indiscriminating Sun, I can shade myself and read my book. And listening to this water's pretty voices I invent for it exquisite epithets, calling it *silver-clean* or *moss-margined* or *nymph-frequented*, and idly promise to place it among the learned fountains and pools of the world, making of it a cool green thought for English exiles in the dust and glare of Eastern deserts.

## The Spider

What shall I compare it to, this fantastic thing I call my Mind? To a waste-paper basket, to a sieve choked with sediment, or to a barrel full of floating froth and refuse?

No, what it is really most like is a spider's web, insecurely hung on leaves and twigs, quivering in every wind, and sprinkled with dewdrops and dead flies. And at its centre, pondering forever the Problem of Existence, sits motionless the spider-like and uncanny Soul.

# BOOK II

*"Thou, Trivia, goddess, aid my song: Through spacious streets conduct thy bard along."*

Gay's *Trivia, or New Art of Walking Streets of London.*

## *L'oiseau Bleu*

What is it, I have more than once asked myself, what is it that I am looking for in my walks about London? Sometimes it seems to me as if I were following a Bird, a bright Bird that sings sweetly as it floats about from one place to another.

When I find myself however among persons of middle age and settled principles, see them moving regularly to their offices—what keeps them going? I ask myself. And I feel ashamed of myself and my Bird.

There is though a Philosophic Doctrine—I studied it at College, and I know that many serious people believe it—which maintains that all men, in spite of appearances and pretensions, all live alike for Pleasure. This theory certainly brings portly, respected persons very near to me. Indeed with a sense of low complicity I have sometimes followed and watched a Bishop. Was he too on the hunt for Pleasure, solemnly pursuing his Bird?

## *At The Bank*

Entering the Bank in a composed manner, I drew a cheque and handed it to the cashier through the grating. Then I eyed him narrowly. Would not that astute official see that I was only posing as a Real Person? No; he calmly opened a little drawer, took out some real sovereigns, counted them carefully, and handed them to me in a brass-tipped shovel. I went away feeling I had perpetrated a delightful fraud. I had got some of the gold of the actual world!

Yet now and then, at the sight of my name on a visiting card, or of my face photographed in a group among other faces, or when I see a letter addressed in my hand, or catch the sound of my own voice, I grow shy in the presence of a mysterious Person who is myself, is known by my name, and who apparently does exist. Can it be possible that I am as real as any one else, and that all of us—the cashier and banker at the Bank, the King on his throne—all feel ourselves like ghosts and goblins in this authentic world?

## *Mammon*

Moralists and Church Fathers have named it the root of all Evil, the begetter of hate and bloodshed, the sure cause of the soul's damnation. It has been called "trash," "muck," "dunghill excrement," by grave authors. The love of it is denounced in all Sacred Writings; we find it reprehended on Chaldean bricks, and in the earliest papyri. Buddha, Confucius, Christ, set their faces against it; and they have been followed in more modern times by beneficed Clergymen, Sunday School Teachers, and the leaders of the Higher Thought. But have the condemnations of all the ages done anything to tarnish that bright lustre? Men dig for it ever deeper into the earth's intestines, travel in search of it farther and farther to arctic and unpleasant regions.

In spite of all my moral reading, I must confess that I like to have some of this gaudy substance in my pocket. Its presence cheers and comforts me, diffuses a genial warmth through my body. My eyes rejoice in the shine of it; its clinquant sound is music in my ears. Since I then am in his paid service, and reject none of the doles of his bounty, I too dwell in the House of Mammon. I bow before the Idol, and taste the unhallowed ecstasy.

How many Altars have been overthrown, and how many Theologies and heavenly Dreams have had their bottoms knocked out of them, while He has sat there, a great God, golden and adorned, and secure on His unmoved throne?

*I See the World*

"But you go nowhere, see nothing of the world," my cousins said. Now though I do go sometimes to the parties to which I am now and then invited, I find, as a matter of fact, that I get really much more pleasure by looking in at windows, and have a way of my own of seeing the World. And of summer evenings, when motors hurry through the late twilight, and the great houses take on airs of inscrutable expectation, I go owling out through the dusk; and wandering toward the West, lose my way in unknown streets—an unknown City of revels. And when a door opens and a bediamonded Lady moves to her motor over carpets unrolled by powdered footmen, I can easily think her some great Courtezan, or some half-believed Duchess, hurrying to card-tables and lit candles and strange scenes of joy. I like to see that there are still splendid people on this flat earth; and at dances, standing in the street with the crowd, and stirred by the music, the lights, the rushing sound of voices, I think the Ladies as beautiful as Stars who move up those lanes of light past our rows of vagabond faces; the young men look like Lords in novels; and if (it has once or twice happened) people I know go by me, they strike me as changed and rapt beyond my sphere. And when on hot nights windows are left open, and I can look in at Dinner Parties, as I peer through lace curtains and window-flowers at the silver, the women's shoulders, the shimmer of their jewels, and the divine attitudes of their heads as they lean and listen, I imagine extraordinary intrigues and unheard of wines and passions.

*Social Success*

The servant gave me my coat and hat, and in a glow of self-satisfaction I walked out into the night. "A delightful evening," I reflected, "the nicest kind of people. What I said about finance and French philosophy impressed them; and how they laughed when I imitated a pig squealing."

But soon after, "God, it's awful," I muttered, "I wish I were dead."

*Apotheosis*

But Oh, those heavenly moments when I feel this trivial universe too small to contain my Attributes; when a sense of the divine Ipseity invades me; when I know that my voice is the voice of Truth, and my umbrella God's umbrella!

*The Spring in London*

London seemed last winter like an underground city; as if its low sky were the roof of a cave, and its murky day a light such as one reads of in countries beneath the earth.

And yet the natural sunlight sometimes shone there; white clouds voyaged in the blue sky; the interminable multitudes of roofs were washed with silver by the Moon, or cloaked with a mantle of new-fallen snow. And the coming of Spring to London was to me not unlike the descent of the maiden-goddess into Death's Kingdoms, when pink almond blossoms blew about her in the gloom, and those shadowy people were stirred with faint longings for meadows and the shepherd's life. Nor was there anything more virginal and fresh in wood or orchard than the shimmer of young foliage, which, in May, dimmed with delicate green all the smoke-blackened London trees.

*Fashion Plates*

I like loitering at the bookstalls, looking in at the windows of printshops, and romancing over the pictures I see of shepherdesses and old-fashioned Beauties. Tall and slim and crowned with plumes in one period, in another these Ladies become as wide-winged as butterflies, or float, large, balloon-like visions, down summer streets. And yet in all shapes they have always (I tell myself) created thrilling effects of beauty, and waked in the breasts of modish young men ever the same charming Emotion.

But then I have questioned this. Is the emotion always precisely the same? Is it true to say that the human heart remains quite unchanged beneath all the changing fashions of frills and ruffles? In this elegant and cruel Sentiment, I rather fancy that colour and shape do make a difference. I have a notion that about 1840 was the Zenith, the Meridian Hour, the Golden Age of the Passion. Those tight-waisted, whiskered Beaux, those crinolined Beauties, adored one another, I believe, with a leisure, a refinement, and dismay not quite attainable at other dates.

*Mental Vice*

There are certain hackneyed Thoughts that will force them-selves on me; I find my mind, especially in hot weather, infested and buzzed about by moral Platitudes. "That shows—" I say to myself, or, "How true it is—" or, "I really ought to have known!" The sight of a large clock sets me off into musings on the flight of Time; a steamer on the Thames or lines of telegraph inevitably suggest the benefits of Civilization, man's triumph over Nature, the heroism of Inventors, the courage, amid ridicule and poverty, of Stephenson and Watt. Like faint, rather unpleasant smells, these thoughts lurk about railway stations. I can hardly post a letter without marvelling at the excellence and accuracy of the Postal System.

Then the pride in the British Constitution and British Freedom, which comes over me when I see, even in the distance, the Towers of Westminster Palace—that Mother of Parliaments—it is not much comfort that this should be chastened, as I walk down the Embankment, by the sight of Cleopatra's Needle, and the Thought that it will no doubt witness the Fall of the British, as it has that of other Empires, remaining to point its Moral, as old as Egypt, to Antipodeans musing on the dilapidated bridges.

I am sometimes afraid of finding that there is a moral for everything; that the whole great frame of the Universe has a key, like a box; has been contrived and set going by a well-meaning but humdrum Eighteenth-century Creator. It would be a kind of Hell, surely, a world in which everything could be at once explained, shown to be obvious and useful. I am sated with Lesson and Allegory, weary of monitory ants, industrious bees, and preaching animals. The benefits of Civilization cloy me. I have seen enough shining of the didactic Sun.

So gazing up on hot summer nights at the London stars, I cool my thoughts with a vision of the giddy, infinite, meaningless waste of Creation, the blazing Suns, the Planets and frozen Moons, all crashing blindly forever across the void of space.

*The Organ of Life*

Almost always In London—in the congregated uproar of streets, or in the noise that drifts through wails and windows—you can hear the hackneyed melancholy of street music; a music which sounds like the actual voice of the human Heart, singing the lost joys, the regrets, the loveless lives of the people who blacken the pavements, or jolt along on the busses.

"Speak to me kindly," the hand-organ implores; "I'm all alone!" it screams amid the throng; "thy Vows are all broken," it laments in dingy courtyards, "And light is thy Fame." And of hot summer afternoons, the Cry for Courage to Remember, or Calmness to Forget, floats in with the smell of paint and asphalt—faint and sad—-through open office windows.

*Humiliation*

"My own view is," I began, but no one listened. At the next pause, "I always say," I remarked, but again the loud talk went on. Someone told a story. When the laughter had ended, "I often think—"; but looking round the table I could catch no friendly or attentive eye. It was humiliating, but more humiliating the thought that Sophocles and Goethe would have always commanded attention, while the lack of it would not have troubled Spinoza or Abraham Lincoln.

## Green Ivory

What a bore it is, waking up in the morning always the same person. I wish I were unflinching and emphatic, and had big, bushy eyebrows and a Message for the Age. I wish I were a deep Thinker, or a great Ventriloquist.

I should like to be refined and melancholy, the victim of a hopeless passion; to love in the old, stilted way, with impossible Adoration and Despair under the pale-faced Moon.

I wish I could get up; I wish I were the world's greatest Violinist. I wish I had lots of silver, and first Editions, and green ivory.

## In The Park

"Yes," I said one afternoon in the Park, as I looked rather contemptuously at the people of Fashion, moving slow and well-dressed in the sunshine, "but how about the others, the Courtiers and Beauties and Dandies of the past? They wore fine costumes, and glittered for their hour in the summer air. What has become of them?" I somewhat rhetorically asked. They were all dead now. Their day was over. They were cold in their graves.

And I thought of those severe spirits who, in garrets far from the Park and Fashion, had scorned the fumes and tinsel of the noisy World.

But, good Heavens! these severe spirits were, it occurred to me, all, as a matter of fact, quite as dead as the others.

## The Correct

I am sometimes visited by a suspicion that everything isn't quite all right with the Righteous; that the Moral Law speaks in muffled and dubious tones to those who listen most scrupulously for its dictates. I feel sure I have detected a look of doubt and misgiving in the eyes of its earnest upholders.

But there is no such shadow or cloud on the faces in Club windows, or in the eyes of drivers of four-in-hands, or of fashionable young men walking down Piccadilly. For these live by a Rule which has not been drawn down from far-off and questionable skies, and needs no sanction; what they do is Correct, and that is all. Correctly dressed from head to foot, they pass, with correct speech and thoughts and gestures, correctly across the roundness of the Earth.

## "Where Do I Come In?"

When I read in the *Times* about India and all its problems and populations; when I look at the letters in large type of important personages, and find myself face to face with the Questions, Movements, and great Activities of the Age, "Where do I come in?" I ask myself uneasily.

Then in the great *Times*-reflected world I find the corner where I play my humble but necessary part. For I am one of the unpraised, unrewarded millions without whom Statistics would be a bankrupt science. It is we who are born, who marry, who die, in constant ratios; who regularly lose so many umbrellas, post just so many unaddressed letters every year. And there are enthusiasts among us who, without the least thought of their own convenience, allow omnibuses to run over them; or throw themselves month by month, in fixed numbers, from the London bridges.

## Microbes

But how Is one to keep free from those mental microbes that worm-eat people's brains—those Theories and Diets and Enthusiasms and infectious Doctrines that we are always liable to catch from what seem the most innocuous contacts? People go about laden with germs; they breathe creeds and convictions on you whenever they open their mouths. Books and newspapers are simply creeping with them—the monthly Reviews seem to have room for nothing else. Wherewithal then shall a young man cleanse his way; and how shall he keep his mind immune to Theosophical speculations, and novel schemes of Salvation?

Can he ever be sure that he won't be suddenly struck down by the fever of Funeral, or of Spelling Reform, or take to his bed with a new Sex Theory?

But is this struggle for a healthy mind in a maggoty universe really after all worth it? Are there not soporific dreams and sweet deliriums more soothing than Reason? If Transmigration can make clear the dark Problem of Evil; if Mrs. Mary Baker Eddy can free us from the dominion of Death; if the belief that Bacon wrote Shakespeare gives a peace that the world cannot give, why pedantically reject such kindly solace? Why not be led with the others by still waters, and be made to lie down in green pastures?

## The Quest

"We walk alone in the world," the Moralist, at the end of his essay on Ideal Friendship, writes somewhat sadly, "Friends such as we desire are dreams and fables," Yet we never quite give up the hope of finding them. But what awful things happen to us? what snubs, what set-downs we experience, what shames and disillusions. We can never really tell what these new unknown persons may do to us. Sometimes they seem nice, and then begin to talk like gramophones. Sometimes they grab at us with moist hands, or breathe hotly on our necks, or make awful confidences, or drench us from sentimental slop-pails. And too often, among the thoughts in the loveliest heads, we come on nests of woolly caterpillars.

And yet we brush our hats, pull on our gloves, and go out and ring door-bells.

## The Kaleidoscope

I find in my mind, in its miscellany of ideas and musings, a curious collection of little landscapes and pictures, shining and fading for no reason. Sometimes they are views in no way remarkable-the corner of a road, a heap of stones, an old gate. But there are many charming pictures, too: as I read, between my eyes and book, the Moon sheds down on harvest fields her chill of silver; I see autumnal avenues, with the leaves falling, or swept in heaps; and storms blow among my thoughts, with the rain beating forever on the fields. Then Winter's upward glare of snow appears; or the pink and delicate green of Spring in the windy sunshine; or cornfields and green waters, and youths bathing in Summer's golden heats.

And as I walk about, certain places haunt me: a cathedral rises above a dark blue foreign town, the colour of ivory in the sunset light; now I find myself in a French garden full of lilacs and bees, and shut-in sunshine, with the Mediterranean lounging and washing outside its walls; now in a little college library, with busts, and the green reflected light of Oxford lawns—and again I hear the bells, reminding me of the familiar Oxford hours.

## Oxford Street

One late winter afternoon in Oxford Street, amid the noise of vehicles and voices that filled that dusky thoroughfare, as I was borne onward with the crowd past the great electric-lighted shops, a holy Indifference filled my thoughts. Illusion had faded from me; I was not touched by any desire for the goods displayed in those golden windows, nor had I the smallest share in the appetites and fears of all those moving and anxious faces. And as I listened with Asiatic detachment to the London traffic, its sound changed into something ancient and dissonant and sad—into the turbid flow of that stream of Craving which sweeps men onward through the meaningless cycles of Existence, blind and enslaved forever. But I had reached the farther shore, the Harbour of Deliverance, the Holy City; the Great Peace beyond all this turmoil and fret compassed me around. *Om Mani padme hum*—I murmured the sacred syllables, smiling with the pitying smile of the Enlightened One on his heavenly lotus.

Then, in a shop-window, I saw a neatly fitted suit-case. I liked that suit-case; I desired to possess it. Immediately I was enveloped by the mists of Illusion, chained once more to the Wheel of Existence, whirled onward along Oxford Street in that turbid stream of wrong-belief, and lust, and sorrow, and anger.

32

## Beauty

Among all the ugly mugs of the world we see now and then a face made after the divine pattern. Then, a wonderful thing happens to us; the Blue Bird sings, the golden Splendour shines, and for a queer moment everything seems meaningless save our impulse to follow those fair forms, to follow them to the clear Paradises they promise.

Plato assures us that these moments are not (as we are apt to think them) mere blurs and delusions of the senses, but divine revelations; that in a lovely face we see imaged, as in a mirror, the Absolute Beauty—; it is Reality, flashing on us in the cave where we dwell amid shadows and darkness. Therefore we should follow these fair forms, and their shining footsteps will lead us upward to the highest heaven of Wisdom. The Poets, too, keep chanting this great doctrine of Beauty in grave notes to their golden strings. Its music floats up through the skies so sweet, so strange, that the very Angels seem to lean from their stars to listen.

But, O Plato, O Shelley, O Angels of Heaven, what scrapes you do get us into!

## The Power of Words

I thanked the club porter who helped me into my coat, and stepped out lightly into the vastness and freshness of the Night. And as I walked along my eyes were dazzling with the glare I had left; I still seemed to hear the sound of my speech, and the applause and laughter.

And when I looked up at the Stars, the great Stars that bore me company, streaming over the dark houses as I moved, I felt that I was the Lord of Life; the mystery and disquieting meaninglessness of existence—the existence of other people, and of my own, were solved for me now. As for the Earth, hurrying beneath my feet, how bright was its journey; how shining the goal toward which it went swinging—you might really say leaping—through the sky.

"I must tell the Human Race of this!" I heard my voice; saw my prophetic gestures, as I expounded the ultimate meaning of existence to the white, rapt faces of Humanity. Only to find the words—that troubled me; were there then no words to describe this Vision—divine—intoxicating?

And then the Word struck me; the Word people would use. I stopped in the street; my Soul was silenced like a bell that snarls at a jarring touch. I stood there awhile and meditated on language, its perfidious meanness, the inadequacy, the ignominy of our vocabulary, and how Moralists have spoiled our words by distilling into them, as into little vials of poison, all their hatred of human joy. Away with that police-force of brutal words which bursts in on our best moments and arrests our finest feelings! This music within me, large, like the song of the stars—like a Glory of Angels singing—"No one has any right to say I am drunk!" I shouted.

## Self-Analysis

"Yes, aren't they odd, the thoughts that float through one's mind for no reason? But why not be frank—I suppose the best of us are shocked at times by the things we find ourselves thinking. Don't you agree," I went on, not noticing (until it was too late) that all other conversation had ceased, and the whole dinner-party was listening, "don't you agree that the oddest of all are the improper thoughts that come into one's head—the unspeakable words I mean, and Obscenities?" When I remember that remark, I hasten to enlarge my mind with ampler considerations. I think of Space, and the unimportance in its unmeasured vastness, of our toy solar system; I lose myself in speculations on the lapse of Time, reflecting how at the best our human life on this minute and perishing planet is as brief as a dream.

## The Voice of the World

"And what are you doing now?" The question of these school contemporaries of mine, and their greeting the other day in Piccadilly (I remember how shabby I felt as I stood talking to them)—for a day or two that question haunted me. And behind their well-bred voices I seemed to hear the voice of Schoolmasters and Tutors, of the Professional Classes, and indeed of all the world. What, as a plain matter of fact, was I doing, how did I spend my days? The life-days which I knew were numbered, and which were described in sermons and on tombstones as so irrevocable, so melancholy-brief.

I decided to change my life. I too would be somebody in my time and age; my contemporaries should treat me as an important person. I began thinking of my endeavours, my studies by the midnight lamp, my risings at dawn for stolen hours of self-improvement.

But alas, the day, the little day, was enough just then. It somehow seemed enough, just to be alive in the Spring, with the young green of the trees, the smell of smoke in the sunshine; I loved the old shops and books, the uproar darkening and brightening in the shabby daylight. Just a run of good-looking faces—and I was always looking for faces—would keep me amused. And London was but a dim-lit stage on which I could play in fancy any part I liked. I woke up in the morning like Byron to find myself famous; I was drawn like Chatham to St. Paul's, amid the cheers of the Nation, and sternly exclaimed with Cromwell, "Take away that bauble," as I sauntered past the Houses of Parliament.

## And Anyhow

And anyhow, soon, so soon (in only seven million years or thereabouts the Encyclopaedia said) this Earth would grow cold, all human activities end, and the last wretched mortals freeze to death in the dim rays of the dying Sun.

## Drawbacks

34

I should be all right.... If it weren't for these sudden visitations of Happiness, these downpourings of Heaven's blue, little invasions of Paradise, or waftings to the Happy Islands, or whatever you may call these disconcerting Moments, I should be like everybody else, and as blameless a rate-payer as any in our Row.

*Talk*

Once in a while, when doors are closed and curtains drawn on a group of free spirits, the miracle happens, and Good Talk begins. 'Tis a sudden illumination—the glow, it may be of sanctified candles, or, more likely, the blaze around a cauldron of gossip.

Is there an ecstasy or any intoxication like it? Oh? to talk, to talk people into monsters, to talk one's self out of one's clothes, to talk God from His heaven, and turn everything in the world into a bright tissue of phrases!

These Pentecosts and outpourings of the spirit can only occur very rarely, or the Universe itself would be soon talked out of existence.

*The Church of England*

I have my Anglican moments; and as I sat there that Sunday afternoon, in the Palladian interior of the London Church, and listened to the unexpressive voices chanting the correct service, I felt a comfortable assurance that we were in no danger of being betrayed into any unseemly manifestations of religious fervour. We had not gathered together at that performance to abase ourselves with furious hosannas before any dark Creator of an untamed Universe, no Deity of freaks and miracles and sinister hocus-pocus; but to pay our duty to a highly respected Anglican First Cause—undemonstrative, gentlemanly and conscientious—whom, without loss of self-respect, we could sincerely and decorously praise.

*Misgiving*

We were talking of people, and a name familiar to us all was mentioned. We paused and looked at each other; then soon, by means of anecdotes and clever touches, that personality was reconstructed, and seemed to appear before us, large, pink, and life-like, and gave a comic sketch of itself with appropriate poses.

"Of course," I said to myself, "this sort of thing never happens to me." For the notion was quite unthinkable, the notion I mean of my own dear image, called up like this without my knowledge, to turn my discreet way of life into a cake-walk.

*Sanctuaries*

She said, "How small the world is after all!"

I thought of China, of a holy mountain in the West of China, full of legends and sacred trees and demon-haunted caves. It is always enveloped in mountain mists; and in that white thick air I heard the faint sound of bells, and the muffled footsteps of innumerable pilgrims, and the reiterated mantra, *Nam-Mo, O-mi-to-Fo*, which they murmur as they climb its slopes. High up among its temples and monasteries marched processions of monks, with intoned services, and many prostrations, and lighted candles that glimmer through the fog. There in their solemn shrines stood the statues of the Arahats, and there, seated on his white elephant, loomed immense and dim, the image of Amitabha, the Lord of the Western Heavens.

She said "Life is so complicated!" Climbing inaccessible cliffs of rock and ice, I shut myself within a Tibetan monastery beyond the Himalayan ramparts. I join with choirs of monks, intoning their deep sonorous dirges and unintelligible prayers; I beat drums, I clash cymbals, and blow at dawn from the Lamasery roofs conches, and loud discordant trumpets. And wandering through those vast and shadowy halls, as I tend the butter-lamps of the golden Buddhas, and watch the storms that blow across the barren mountains, I taste an imaginary bliss, and then pass on to other scenes and incarnations along the endless road that leads me to Nirvana.

"But I do wish you would tell me what you really think?"

I fled to Africa, into the depths of the dark Ashanti forest. There, in its gloomiest recesses, where the soil is stained with the blood of the negroes He has eaten, dwells that monstrous Deity of human shape and red colour, the great Fetish God, Sasabonsum. I like Sasabonsum: other Gods are sometimes moved to pity and forgiveness, but to Him such weakness is unknown. He is utterly and absolutely implacable; no gifts or prayers, no holocausts of human victims can appease, or ever, for one moment, propitiate Him.

*Symptoms*

"But there are certain people I simply cannot stand. A dreariness and sense of death come over me when I meet them—I really find it difficult to breathe when they are in the room, as if they had pumped all the air out of it. Wouldn't it be dreadful to produce that effect on people! But they never seem to be aware of it. I remember once meeting a famous Bore; I really must tell you about it, it shows the unbelievable obtuseness of such people."

I told this and another story or two with great gusto, and talked on of my experiences and sensations, till suddenly I noticed, in the appearance of my charming neighbour, something—a slightly glazed look in her eyes, a just perceptible irregularity in her breathing—which turned that occasion for me into a kind of Nightmare.

*Shadowed*

I sometimes feel a little uneasy about that imagined self of mine—the Me of my daydreams—who leads a melodramatic life of his own, quite unrelated to my real existence. So one day I shadowed him down the street. He loitered along for a while, and then stood at a shop-window and dressed himself out in a gaudy tie and yellow waistcoat. Then he bought a great sponge and two stuffed birds and took them to lodgings, where he led for a while a shady existence. Next he moved to a big house in Mayfair, and gave grand dinner-parties, with splendid service and costly wines. His amorous adventures in this region I pass over. He soon sold his house and horses, gave up his motors, dismissed his retinue of servants, and went—saving two young ladies from being run over on the way—to live a life of heroic self-sacrifice among the poor.

I was beginning to feel encouraged about him, when in passing a fishmonger's, he pointed at a great salmon and said, "I caught that fish."

*The Incredible*

"Yes, but they were rather afraid of you."

"Afraid of *me*?"

"Yes, so one of them told me afterwards."

I was fairly jiggered. If my personality can inspire fear or respect the world must be a simpler place than I had thought it. Afraid of a shadow, a poor make-believe like me? Are children more absurdly terrified by a candle in a hollow turnip? Was Bedlam at full moon ever scared by anything half so silly?

*Terror*

A pause suddenly fell on our conversation—one of those uncomfortable lapses when we sit with fixed smiles, searching our minds for some remark with which to fill up the unseasonable silence. It was only a moment—"But suppose," I said to myself with horrible curiosity, "suppose none of us had found a word to say, and we had gone on sitting in silence?"

It is the dread of Something happening, Something unknown and awful, that makes us do anything to keep the flicker of talk from dying out. So travellers at night in an unknown forest keep their fires ablaze, in fear of Wild Beasts lurking ready in the darkness to leap upon them.

*Pathos*

When winter twilight falls on my street with the rain, a sense of the horrible sadness of life descends upon me. I think of drunken old women who drown themselves because nobody loves them; I think of Napoleon at St. Helena, and of Byron growing morose and fat in the enervating climate of Italy.

## Inconstancy

The rose that one wears and throws away, the friend one forgets, the music that passes—out of the well-known transitoriness of mortal things I have made myself a maxim or precept to the effect that it is foolish to look for one face, or to listen long for one voice, in a world that is after all, as I know, full of enchanting voices.

But all the same, I can never quite forget the enthusiasm with which, as a boy, I read the praises of Constancy and True Love, and the unchanged Northern Star.

## The Poplar

There is a great tree in Sussex, whose cloud of thin foliage floats high in the summer air. The thrush sings in it, and blackbirds, who fill the late, decorative sunshine with a shimmer of golden sound. There the nightingale finds her green cloister; and on those branches sometimes, like a great fruit, hangs the lemon-coloured Moon. In the glare of August, when all the world is faint with heat, there is always a breeze in those cool recesses, always a noise, like the noise of water, among its lightly hung leaves.

But the owner of this Tree lives in London, reading books.

## On the Doorstep

I rang the bell as of old; as of old I gazed at the great shining Door and waited. But, alas! that flutter and beat of the wild heart, that delicious doorstep Terror—it was gone; and with it dear, fantastic, panic-stricken Youth had rung the bell, flitted round the corner and vanished for ever.

## Old Clothes

Shabby old waistcoat, what made the heart beat that you used to cover? Funny-shaped hat, where are the thoughts that once nested beneath you? Old shoes, hurrying along what dim paths of the Past did I wear out your sole-leather?

## Youth

Oh dear, this living and eating and growing old; these doubts and aches in the back, and want of interest in the Moon and Roses...

Am I the person who used to wake in the middle of the night and laugh with the joy of living? Who worried about the existence of God, and danced with young ladies till long after daybreak? Who sang "Auld Lang Syne" and howled with sentiment, and more than once gazed at the summer stars through a blur of great, romantic tears?

## Consolation

The other day, depressed on the Underground, I tried to cheer myself by thinking over the joys of our human lot. But there wasn't one of them for which I seemed to care a hang—not Wine, nor Friendship, nor Eating, nor Making Love, nor the Consciousness of Virtue. Was it worth while then going up in a lift into a world that had nothing less trite to offer?

Then I thought of reading—the nice and subtle happiness of reading. This was enough, this joy not dulled by Age, this polite and unpunished vice, this selfish, serene, life-long intoxication.

## Sir Eustace Carr

When I read the news about Sir Eustace Carr in the morning paper, I was startled, like everyone else who knew, if only by name this young man, whose wealth and good looks, whose adventurous travels and whose brilliant and happy marriage, had made of him an almost romantic figure.

Every now and then one hears of some strange happening of this kind. But they are acts so anomalous, in such startling contradiction to all our usual ways and accepted notions of life and its value, that most of us are willing enough to accept the familiar explanation of insanity, or any other commonplace cause which may be alleged—financial trouble, or some passionate entanglement, and the fear of scandal and exposure. And then the Suicide is forgotten as soon as possible, and his memory shuffled out of the way as something unpleasant to think of. But with a curiosity that is perhaps a little morbid, I sometimes let my thoughts dwell on these cases, wondering whether the dead man may not have carried to the grave with him the secret of some strange perplexity, some passion or craving or irresistible impulse, of which perhaps his intimates, and certainly the coroner's jury, can have had no inkling.

I had never met or spoken to Sir Eustace Carr—the worlds we lived in were very different—but I had read of his explorations in the East, and of the curious tombs he had discovered—somewhere, was it not?—in the Nile Valley. Then too it happened (and this was the main cause of my interest) that at one time I had seen him more than once, under circumstances that were rather unusual. And now I began to think of this incident. In away it was nothing, and yet the impression haunted me that it was somehow connected with this final act, for which no explanation, beyond that of sudden mental derangement, had been offered. This explanation did not seem to me wholly adequate, although it had been accepted, I believe, both by his friends and the general public—and with the more apparent reason on account of a strain of eccentricity, amounting in some cases almost to insanity, which could be traced, it was said, in his mother's family.

I found it not difficult to revive with a certain vividness the memory of those cold and rainy November weeks that I had happened to spend alone, some years ago, in Venice, and of the churches which I had so frequently haunted. Especially I remembered the great dreary church in the piazza near my lodgings, into which I would often go on my way to my rooms in the twilight. It was the season when all the Venice churches are draped in black, and services for the dead are held in them at dawn and twilight; and when I entered this Baroque interior, with its twisted columns and volutes and high-piled, hideous tombs, adorned with skeletons and allegorical figures and angels blowing trumpets—all so agitated, and yet all so dead and empty and frigid—I would find the fantastic darkness filled with glimmering candles, and kneeling figures, and the discordant noise of chanting. There I would sit, while outside night fell with the rain on Venice; the palaces and green canals faded into darkness, and the great bells, swinging against the low sky, sent the melancholy sound of their voices far over the lagoons.

It was here, in this church, that I used to see Sir Eustace Carr; would generally find him in the same corner when I entered, and would sometimes watch his face, until the ceremonious extinguishing of the candles, one by one, left us in shadowy night. It was a handsome and thoughtful face, and I remember more than once wondering what had brought him to Venice in that unseasonable month, and why he came so regularly to this monotonous service. It was as if some spell had drawn him; and now, with my curiosity newly wakened, I asked myself what had been that spell? I also must have been affected by it, for I had been there also in his uncommunicating company. Here, I felt, was perhaps the answer to my question, the secret of the enigma that puzzled me; and as I went over my memories of that time, and revived its sombre and almost sinister fascination, I seemed to see an answer looming before my imagination. But it was an answer, an hypothesis or supposition, so fantastic, that my common sense could hardly accept it.

For I now saw that the spell which had been on us both at that time in Venice had been nothing but the spell and tremendous incantation of the Thought of Death. The dreary city with its decaying palaces and great tomb-encumbered churches had really seemed, in those dark and desolate weeks, to be the home and metropolis of the great King of Terrors; and the services at dawn and twilight, with their prayers for the Dead, and funereal candles, had been the chanted ritual of his worship. Now suppose (such was the notion that held my imagination) suppose this spell, which I had felt but for a time and dimly, should become to someone a real obsession, casting its shadow more and more completely over a life otherwise prosperous and happy, might not this be the clue to a history like that of Sir Eustace Carr's—not only his interest in the buried East, his presence at that time in Venice, but also his unexplained and mysterious end?

Musing on this half-believed notion, I thought of the great personages and great nations we read of in ancient history, who have seemed to live with a kind of morbid pleasure in the shadow of this great Thought; who have surrounded themselves with mementoes of Death, and hideous symbols of its power, and who, like the Egyptians, have found their main interest, not in the present, but in imaginary explorations of the unknown future; not on the sunlit surface of this earth, but in the vaults and dwelling-places of the Dead beneath it.

Since this preoccupation, this curiosity, this nostalgia, has exercised so enormous a fascination in the past, I found it not impossible to imagine some modern favourite of fortune falling a victim to this malady of the soul; until at last, growing weary of other satisfactions, he might be drawn to open for himself the dark portal and join the inhabitants of that dim region, "Kings and Counsellors of the earth, Princes that had gold, who filled their houses with silver." This, as I say, was the notion that haunted me, the link my imagination forged between Sir Eustace Carr's presence in that dark Venetian church, and his self-caused death some years later. But whether it is really a clue to that unexplained mystery, or whether it is nothing more than a somewhat sinister fancy, of course, I cannot say.

*The Lord Mayor*

An arctic wind was blowing; it cut through me as I stood there. The boot-black was finishing his work and complaints.

"But I should be 'appy, sir, if only I could make four bob a day," he said.

I looked down at him; it seemed absurd, the belief of this crippled, half-frozen creature, that four-shillings would make him happy. Happiness! the fabled treasure of some far-away heaven I thought it that afternoon; not to be bought with gold, not of this earth!

I said something to this effect. But four shillings a day was enough for the boot-black.

"Why," he said, "I should be as 'appy as the Lord Mayor!"

*The Burden*

I know too much; I have stuffed too many of the facts of History and Science into my intellectuals. My eyes have grown dim over books; believing in geological periods, cave-dwellers, Chinese Dynasties, and the fixed stars has prematurely aged me.

Why am I to blame for all that is wrong in the world? I didn't invent Sin and Hate and Slaughter. Who made it my duty anyhow to administer the Universe, and keep the planets to their Copernican courses? My shoulders are bent beneath the weight of the firmament; I grow weary of propping up, like Atlas, this vast and erroneous Cosmos.

41

From under the roof of my umbrella I saw the washed pavement lapsing beneath my feet, the news-posters lying smeared with dirt at the crossings, the tracks of the busses in the liquid mud. On I went through this dreary world of wetness. And through how many rains and years shall I still hurry down wet streets—middle-aged, and then, perhaps, very old? And on what errands?

Asking myself this cheerless question I fade from your vision, Reader, into the distance, sloping my umbrella against the wind.

THE END

Made in the USA
Columbia, SC
24 September 2023

23337979R00026